# COLORADO BUCKET LIST TRAVEL GUIDE

Explore the Remarkable State of Colorado and Enjoy an Adventure of a Lifetime (50 Locations/Activities with Full-Color Images)

## SCOTT JACKSON

# Contents

# Introduction

Colorado is an outdoor enthusiast's paradise, full of endless adventure; fresh, crisp air; and over 300 days of sunshine. Beyond its incredibly diverse landscapes ranging from high deserts and alpine tundra to raging rivers, Colorado offers excellent cities to visit, including Denver, Fort Collins, Colorado Springs, and Boulder. Foodies will never run out of options at local farmers markets, restaurants, and world-class breweries that scatter the state. Historians, archaeologists, and children will love visiting the city museums, and exploring Old Western mining towns by rail, fossil sites, and the Ancestral Puebloans sites that dot the region.

Regardless of the season you find yourself in you will likely have your adrenaline pumping for downhill skiing, mountain biking, or driving through the highlands. Trying something new for the first time will not be difficult with options like horseback riding, whitewater rafting, heli-skiing, or fly fishing the Arkansas River. Whether you are a solo traveler looking to scale mountains, a couple seeking a romantic retreat at a dude ranch, or a family wanting to hike with the kids, Colorado has abundant options. Getting high won't be a problem as Colorado is home to the most fourteeners in the nation, with 58 mountain peaks above 14,000 feet above sea level.

While you enjoy all that the Centennial State has to offer, be sure to do so responsibly under the guidelines of Leave No Trace, set by the Colorado Tourism Office.

MAP

We've created an up-to-date map via Google Maps which can be viewed in the link below. We suggest you save it as a way to help plan your trip.

shorturl.at/nKY15

LEAVE NO TRACE

The Colorado Tourism Office joined forces with the Leave No Trace Center for Outdoor Ethics in 2017, making it the first state to do so. Together they created the "Care for Colorado Leave No Trace Principles" and the "Are you Colo-Ready" brochure to help locals and out-of-state visitors preserve and protect the cultural heritage, historic sites, and incredible landscapes.

To learn more, visit The Leave No Trace Center for Outdoor Ethics at https://lnt.org/ and the Colorado Tourism Office website.

7 CARE FOR COLORADO PRINCIPLES

Know before you go: Come prepared and check conditions before going as the weather can be sporadic.

Stick to trails: With nearly 40,000 marked trails and over 13,000 designated campsites, the state has created more than enough space for camping and hiking. Stick to designated areas.

Leave it as you find it: Please leave plants, rocks, and historical artifacts as you find them. Take pictures, not items.

Trash the trash: Pack it in, pack it out! Leave places better than you found them, when possible.

Be careful with fire: Colorado can be very dry, creating dangerous fire conditions. Keep campfires small to avoid wildfires from sparking. Smokers must be mindful of completely putting out their butts and disposing of them properly.

Keep wildlife wild: Colorado is home to tens of thousands of creatures, don't approach them. Don't feed wildlife, and be particularly mindful during spring time when many animals are nesting or coming out of hibernation.

Share our trails and parks: Be considerate of other hikers and keep noise to a minimum when near trails. [1]

ALTITUDE SICKNESS

Colorado's capital is known as the "Mile High City," and correspondingly, the Denver International Airport is situated 5,434 feet above sea level. Given the high altitude, visitors should be mindful of altitude sickness, including dizziness, nausea, and headaches. When visiting Colorado, plan a couple of days to adjust at lower altitudes. While it may be tempting, avoid strenuous exercise upon arrival and limit alcohol intake. As the air is drier, be sure to drink plenty of water.

## MARIJUANA

Colorado has been a receiver of many marijuana tourists since it legalized cannabis in 2012. It is important to note that, at the federal level, cannabis remains illegal, and each state has its own policies. Be mindful of this when stepping onto federal lands with pot. In Colorado, you must be 21 or older to purchase cannabis. While you may smell the aroma of marijuana in many places, public consumption is banned. Consume responsibly.

## RESERVATIONS

Rocky Mountain National Park, Maroon Bells, Mount Evans, and Manitou Incline are all very busy places and should be planned out in advance. Parking can be problematic in many cases. Take hiker shuttles when they are available to avoid parking issues.

## WEATHER AND CLOTHING

On a visit to Colorado, you can expect a variety of weather conditions as their seasons are not the same as elsewhere, given the high altitude. The winter in Colorado tends to last longer. March and April are still winter, and snowfall in May is common. Fall starts in late September. This will also vary based on where you find yourself.

Our recommendation for packing clothes is to bring layers. You may start some days wearing shorts and a t-shirt but end up with long pants, a jacket, and a hat on. Pack both thick and lightweight clothes. Afternoon rains are more frequent in the summer months, so bring a rain jacket as well. For footwear, we recommend a good pair of sandals (bring socks for when it gets cold) and, of course, good waterproof hiking boots.

*Winter: Fleece jacket, long underwear, water-resistant coat, jeans, and snow pants.*

*Spring/Fall: T-shirts, rain jacket, light fleece, jeans, and shorts.*

*Summer: Light jacket, t-shirts or tank tops, shorts, jeans, hiking pants, swimsuit, and warm clothing for camping.*

*–Colorado Tourism Office*

Regardless of the season, if you are moving around in different altitudes and areas, you will need different layers. Focus on bringing layers!

COVID-19 AND TRAVEL RESTRICTIONS

Coming in from overseas? Be sure to check the U.S. travel restrictions for entry at the Centers of Disease Control and Prevention (CDC).

Additionally, the NAFSA (NAFSA: Association of International Educators) website has a page dedicated to tracking U.S. visa and entry restrictions related to COVID-19.

*"Effective January 26 (2020), the Centers of Disease Control and Prevention (CDC) will require all air passengers entering the United States (including U.S. citizens and Legal Permanent Residents) to present a negative COVID-19 test, taken within three calendar days of departure or proof of recovery from the virus within the last 90 days. Airlines must confirm the negative test result or proof of recovery for all passengers two years of age and over prior to boarding. Airlines must deny boarding of passengers who do not provide documentation of a negative test or recovery."*

*–COVID-19 Restrictions on U.S. Visas and Entry, NAFSA*

https://www.nafsa.org/regulatory-information/covid-19-restrictions-us-visas-and-entry

## GETTING IN AND OUT OF COLORADO

Colorado is home to 14 commercial airports, with only one flying internationally. You are likely to fly into Denver International Airport, about an hour away from Colorado Springs to the south and Fort Collins to the north. Boulder is only about a 30-minute drive (depending on traffic). The Rocky Mountains are about an hour and a half away. The farther destinations, such as Durango or Grand Junction, are between four and six hours away.

If you are pressed for time, you can fly into any of the smaller airports from Denver or other destinations in the region. It is possible to skip flying into Denver depending on the time of year and the city you're flying in from.

## DRIVING IN COLORADO

Traffic: Colorado continues to have an influx of inbound migration, causing huge population growth and lagging infrastructure. Those traveling in and out of Denver should be mindful to budget extra time for traffic.

Fast drivers: Coloradans are known to be fast drivers, not just on highways. Colorado has a high speed limit of 75 mph, while many states don't have any over 70 mph. Many roads in the state are considered dangerous when compared to the rest of the nation, given the mountainous and curvy terrain.

Many scenic byways operate by season and are weather dependent. Always check with local authorities on road conditions. 4WD will be necessary for some areas and is noted in the book. Always be sure you've got a full tank, spare food, and extra water in case of emergencies.

Note, hitchhiking is common amongst locals. They're likely just wanting a ride to the top of the mountain.

## Message From The Author

Thank you for choosing this book.

If you find this book to be helpful in any way and would like to show your support, you can do so by leaving a quick review. I personally read all of them and love every time I come across a new one.

Visit the link below to leave a review.

shorturl.at/hipdo

Thank you for your support. I truly hope you enjoy this book. Have fun on your journey!

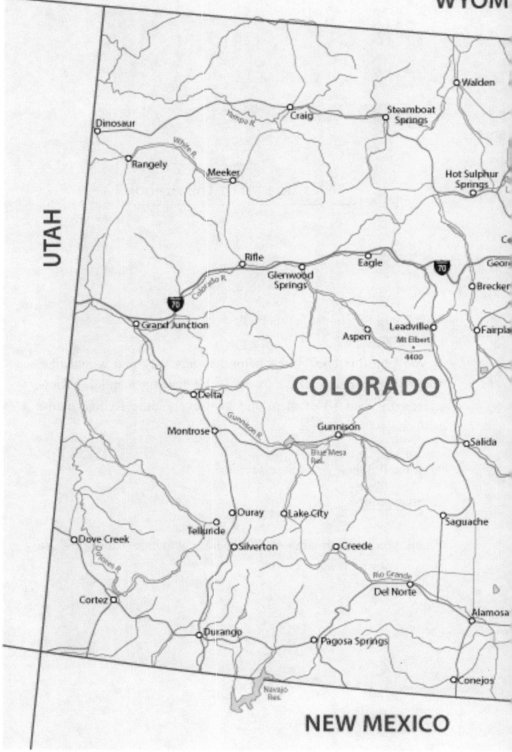

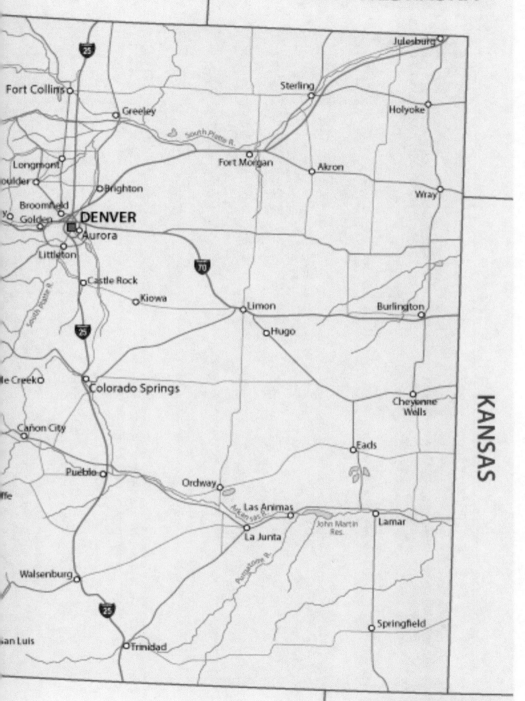

# 1. Rocky Mountain National Park

## NORTHERN COLORADO

Whether you seek an epic multi-day outing or a gentle family-friendly hike, the endless array of trails throughout the 415 square miles that make up the Rocky Mountain National Park has something for everyone. This majestic national park provides a glimpse into the Ice Age, complete with glacier formations and valleys, alpine lakes, and the Colorado River. Getting high won't be a problem with many peaks above 12,000 feet, including Longs Peak towering 14,259 feet.[1]

https://www.nps.gov/romo/index.htm

1000 US Hwy 36, Estes Park, CO 80517

970-586-1206

*Through winter, the Information Office is open 8:00am–4:30pm Mon–Fri.*

*Rocky Mountain National Park is open 24 hours a day, 365 days a year, weather permitting.*

*One-Day Pass: Automobile $25 / Per Person $15 / Motorcycle $25*

*Annual Pass: $70*

While the Rocky Mountain National Park's main draws are its natural heritage and the abundant wildlife such as elk, moose, and bighorn sheep, there are several museums and historic sites. Moraine Park Museum was once the park's welcoming lodge. Built in 1923 by the Civilian Conservation Corps, the building has undergone changes to display the park's geology and wildlife. The entrance is free, and kids will enjoy the interactive exhibits and the nature trail from the gate.

. . .

www.nps.gov

3 Bear Lake Rd, Estes Park, CO 80517

970-586-1363


• • •


From June until October, the Holzwarth Historic Site welcomes visitors to see what life was like over a hundred years ago. In 1916, John and Sophia Holzwarth created a home on 160 acres of the Rockies through the Homestead Act of 1862. This site gives insight into the mountain home of the immigrants.[2]


www.nps.gov

Bear Lake Rd, Estes Park, CO 80517

970-985-1579


Enos Mills Cabin Museum & Gallery provides homage and insight into Enos Mills, the Father of Rocky Mountain National Park. His advocacy for preserving large land areas, scenery, and wildlife is commemorated in the museum. The museum is operated year-round by descendants of Mills and can be visited by appointment only.[3]


www.enosmills.com

6760 CO-7, Estes Park, CO 80517

970-586-4706

4

# 2. Trail Ridge Road

## NORTHERN COLORADO

Also known as the Trail Ridge Road/Beaver Meadow National Scenic Byway, Trail Ridge Road is a stretch of U.S. Hwy. 34 that traverses Rocky Mountain National Park from Estes Park to Grand Lake. The Park Service usually opens the road from Memorial Day weekend until the fall.

. . .

• • •

While traversing the Trail Ridge Road, you may want to drop by the following turnouts for their striking views: Fairview Curve, where you'll see Kawuneeche Valley, a favorite marshy hang-out spot for elk; Milner Pass for a picture of the Rocky Mountains; Continental Divide, Medicine Bow Curve, Alpine Ridge Trail, and Deer Ridge Junction if you want to stop by for a picnic; Rainbow Curve to view the Horseshoe Park; Many Parks Curve to look at several towering peaks. As well the Ute Trail turnout provides history and beautiful views of nearby mountains and Gore Range Overlook offers a view of the beautiful Never Summer Mountains.[4]

Rocky Mountain National Park Information Center

https://www.fhwa.dot.gov/byways/byways/2102

970-586-1206

*Park entrance fees are required. Different fees apply per carload, pedestrian, bicyclist, motorcyclist, or commercial bus.*

# 3. Estes Park

## NORTHERN COLORADO

Estes Park is considered to be a base camp for the Rocky Mountain National Park and is filled with elk, bears, foxes, and other wildlife. Given its proximity to the national park, Estes Park gets crowded in the summer with lodges fully booked, streets lined with RVs, and sidewalks full of tourists. While in Estes Park, it might be a good idea to visit the Colorado Mountain School if you're planning a hike or climb with your family. If you are looking to make multi-day trips into the Rocky Mountain National Park, there are many outdoor gear shops. Lake Estes Trail provides a great 3.5-mile paved pathway that views the lake and the scenic mountain.

If you're interested in knowing about the local culture, the floods that have damaged their town, and its history, check out Estes Park Museum or MacGregor Ranch Museum. From Memorial Day to Labor Day, Estes Park also offers a cable car, Aerial Tramway, which will take you to the top of Prospect Mountain.

There are several ways to get to Estes Park. If you're flying into Denver International Airport, you can take a shuttle service or if you're renting a car, use the toll road (E-470) from the airport to I-25 Northbound. From I-25, you can either take Hwy. 36 or 34 west to Estes Park.

MacGregor Ranch Office

macgregorranch.org

Muriel L. MacGregor Charitable Trust

1301 Clara Dr, Estes Park, CO 80517

970-586-3749

Estes Park Aerial Tramway Terminal

estestram.com

420 E Riverside Dr, Estes Park, Colorado 80517

970-475-4094

*Round-Trip Tickets: Adults $16 / Seniors (60+) $14 / Children (6–11) $10 / Children (5 and under) Free*

# 4. Peak to Peak Scenic Byway

## NORTHERN COLORADO

Titled as Colorado's oldest scenic byway, the Peak to Peak Scenic Byway passes several ghost towns, shows a close-up look of the Continental Divide, and provides spectacular views best seen in the fall season.

. . .

. . .

If you're starting your trip from Boulder, take Canyon Blvd. (Hwy. 119) up through beautiful Boulder Canyon to Nederland, an easy drive on a paved road alongside Boulder Creek that takes you through narrow granite walls (look for rock climbers scaling them above you). Getting from Boulder to Nederland takes about 30 minutes. From Nederland, you can go north (Hwy. 72) to Estes Park or south (Hwy. 119) to the casino towns of Central City and Black Hawk.

The highlight of the byway includes Estes Park, where you'll find many stores and restaurants, not to mention trails that are perfect for mountain biking and horseback riding in the summer. Next is Nederland, the gateway to the Indian Peaks Wilderness Area, a popular hiking and cross-country skiing location. There's also Central City and Black Hawk, former mining towns, which now have several casinos. Located in Central City are the Central City Opera House and the Belvidere Theatre.[35]

# 5. Boulder

## NORTHERN COLORADO

Charmingly called "the city nestled between the mountains and reality," Boulder is 45 minutes away from Denver International Airport. The city is worth a few days to take in the abundance of restaurants, cafes, and breweries in the area. You will inevitably find yourself on Pearl Street's pedestrian walking mall which is filled with something for everyone on its four-block stretch. Shoppers will love the specialty stores, boutiques, and gift shops. Those into the arts will get a thrill out of the numerous galleries, local artisan shops, street performances, and live music that line the street.

Tea fanatics will want to head straight to the Celestial Seasonings Tea Factory, North America's largest manufacturer of herbal teas. They offer free 45-minute factory tours throughout the year, and if you get hungry, breakfast and lunch are available at the Celestial Cafe.

For family-friendly outdoor areas, visit Chautauqua Park and Flatirons. There are several beautiful drives heading out of town, the Peak to Peak Scenic Byway being the most popular. *Note there are separate sections for each of these.

To get to Boulder from Denver International Airport, take Peña Blvd. and merge onto I-70 west. Take I-70 to I-270 west. Continue onto Hwy. 36, which will take you to the east side of Boulder. Other options include taking the public bus and shuttle service. Strolling the city while on foot, on a bus, or on a bike is perfectly viable. Renting a car is also an option, but please note that during the week, there are parking fees downtown.[32] [33]

. . .

Boulder Convention & Visitors Bureau

https://www.bouldercoloradousa.com/

2440 Pearl St, Boulder, CO 80302

303-442-2911

# 6. Flatirons

## NORTHERN COLORADO

The Flatirons consist of five spectacular sandstone formations that make up Boulder's most iconic landmark. Sitting west of the city, the Flatirons give visitors a 45,000-acre recreational space complete with wildlife viewing. Tons of trails scatter the area, with most beginning at the Chautauqua Trailhead, which gets busy during peak seasons.

. . .

Trail difficulty varies. The 2-mile Flatiron Loop Trail is easy to moderate. Royal Arch Trail has a more strenuous 3-mile hike which gives excellent views of Boulder. Check out the Woods Quarry, which provides insight into the sandstone industry for a touch of history. For any maps, closures, and any pertinent information you'll need, swing by the Ranger Cottage.

The Flatirons are also one of the nation's more popular areas for rock climbing. Climbers will enjoy multi-pitch rock climbing routes. While there are a variety of difficulties, introductory courses are offered. Rock climbing outfitters are in abundance in Boulder. Visitors to the Flatirons will tend to be day-trippers from Boulder as there are no sleeping options in the Flatirons area.[34]

As parking is limited during the weekends and peak seasons, we recommend taking the free shuttle from downtown Boulder (or hiker shuttle, ~$3) to the foot of the Flatirons. More info can be found at https://www. bouldercoloradousa.com/ .

# 7. Chautauqua Park

## NORTHERN COLORADO

Popularized initially by Texans looking to escape the hot summers in the late 1800s and early 1900s, Chautauqua Park is a great family outdoor venue. Summers are filled with hiking, while winter gives snow enthusiasts activities such as sledding, snow-shoeing, and sometimes even skiing. What started as a movement in the late 1800s that included a summer school has now transformed into a National Historic Landmark providing year-round activities. Be on the lookout for events throughout the year, most popularly Colorado Music Festival and Art in the Park.

Events and up-to-date transportation info, including a free and paid shuttle option from Boulder to Chautauqua, can be found at https://www.chautauqua.com .

bouldercolorado.gov

Baseline Rd & 9th St, Boulder, CO 80302

303-442-3282

# 8. Fort Collins

## NORTHERN COLORADO

Fort Collins is a vibrant town that centers its culture around its university campuses and 200 miles of bike lanes. The charming old town hosts friendly residents, flowers, street art, cobbled lanes, and historically restored Art Deco buildings. Don't forget to check the local calendar for events such as FoCoMX, the Colorado Brewers' Festival, Tour de Fat, and Bohemian Nights at NewWestFest.[41] History buffs will enjoy the Fort Collins Museum of Discovery which features history, nature, and science exhibits.

Hiking is popular at the Horsetooth Reservoir and Horsetooth Mountain Open Space. From the plains, Horsetooth Rock will be a visible landmark. In the springtime, check out Horsetooth Falls and the spectacular views of the Front Range.

From Fort Collins: From Harmony and Taft Hill Rd., turn west onto County Rd. 38 E. $9 entrance fee per private vehicle.[42]

Horsetooth Mountain Open Space

www.larimer.org

6550 W County Rd 38 E, Fort Collins, CO 80526

970-498-7000

Fort Collins, CO

www.fcgov.com

For some rugged wilderness, check out the scenic Lory State Park, just west of Fort Collins. Four coves are designated swimming areas and there is a bike park with 26 miles of trails, rock climbing, and an equestrian course.[43]

• • •

Lory State Park

708 Lodgepole Dr, Bellvue, CO 80512

303-493-1623

## 9. New Belgium Brewing Company

### NORTHERN COLORADO

Colorado is a haven for craft beer. The most popular brewery is the New Belgium Brewing Company. Founded by Jeff Lebesch and Kim Jordan in 1991, the brewery emphasizes its eco-friendly ethos and is a leader in sustainability and social responsibility. The brewery's flagship beer is the Fat Tire Amber Ale and there is a line of other beers, most popularly the Voodoo Ranger IPA, Mural Agua Fresca Cerveza, and La Folie Sour Brown Ale.


• • •


newbelgium.com

500 Linden St, Fort Collins, CO 80524

970-221-0524

*Opens at 12:00pm*

*Service options: Curbside pickup and no-contact delivery. Currently no dine-in.*


Missed New Belgium Brewery Company in Fort Collins? There's one in the Denver International Airport.


Concourse B, Gate A32, 8500 Peña Blvd, Denver, CO 80249

*6:00am–10:00pm*

# 10. Cache La Pouder River

## NORTHERN COLORADO

With the name translated as Hide the Powder, Cache la Poudre River got its name when French-Canadian trappers hid their gunpowder during a raging blizzard in the early 1800s. Now, the Poudre is Colorado's only nationally designated "Wild & Scenic"

river and a popular summer destination for fly fishing, whitewater rafting, tubing, and kayaking in the Poudre Canyon.[44]

• • •

You can explore the Cache la Poudre River National Heritage Area (CALA) via walking and biking tours near parks, lakes, the Poudre River Trail, and numerous historical sites. The river is also great for whitewater rafting. It's recommended to check with experienced guide services or the United States Forest Service before going in. During summer, drop by Mishawaka Amphitheatre, where they play reggae, bluegrass, and folk music.

Getting to Cache La Poudre River is easiest by car. From Fort Collins, take U.S. Hwy. 287 northwest to its intersection with Colorado Hwy. 14 in Bellevue. From there, the highway proceeds up the rugged Cache la Poudre River Canyon.

www.fcgov.com

201 E Vine Dr, Fort Collins, CO 80524

970-221-6660

# 11. Steamboat Springs

## NORTHERN COLORADO

An internationally known winter ski destination, the Steamboat Springs ski area is considered one of the best in the western United States. Steamboat Mountain Resort has 165 trails and boasts excellent powder. During summer, the mountain resort turns into a bike park featuring 50+ miles of downhill and freeride bike terrain for all ability levels.

Steamboat Ski Resort

www.steamboat.com

• • •

2305 Mt Werner Cir, Steamboat Springs, CO 80487

970-879-6111

Budget travelers will prefer the Howelsen Hill Ski Area. The affordable space is Colorado's oldest continuously operated ski area dating back to 1915. It is the largest natural ski jumping complex and training ground for many Olympians. 21 km of Nordic Trails surround the area.[38]

Howelsen Hill Ski Area

steamboatsprings.net

Howelsen Pkwy, Steamboat Springs, CO 80487

970-879-8499

The Yampa Valley and surrounding area contain several geothermal hot springs. The Strawberry Park Hot Springs are outside the city limits, complete with pools, lodging, and a spa. It also has excellent stargazing opportunities due to the lack of ambient light. In the middle of the town is Old Town Hot Springs which has comparably warmer water than other springs in the area. It offers multiple pools and slides, and according to the Utes, the mineral water has special healing powers.[39]

Old Town Hot Springs

www.oldtownhotsprings.org

136 S Lincoln Ave, Steamboat Springs, CO 80487

970-879-1828

*Guest Rate (includes hot springs, fitness center, and climbing wall): Adults (15+) $25 / Youth (3–14) $19 / Seniors (65+) $22 / Children (under 2 years) Free*

Strawberry Park Hot Springs

strawberryhotsprings.com

44200 Country Rd 36, Steamboat Springs, CO 80487

970-879-0342

*Pool Admission: $20 per person, all ages *Cash or check only. No credit cards.*

Some of the most memorable events in Steamboat Springs include the Hot Air Balloon Festival and Art in the Park in mid-July, the

Strings Music Festival throughout summer, and the First Friday Art Walk on the first Friday of the month.

It's easy to get to Steamboat Springs. If you're driving from Denver, take Rabbit Ears Pass on Hwy. 40. The closest airport is Yampa Valley Regional Airport, 22 miles west of Steamboat. There are shuttle services that can take you to or from the airport. While in Steamboat Springs, there are bus routes, but locals mostly bike, especially in the summer.

Steamboat Springs, CO

www.ci.steamboat.co.us

# 12. Fish Creek Falls

## NORTHERN COLORADO

Fish Creek Canyon is home to the beautiful 280 foot Fish Creek Falls. Mere minutes from downtown Steamboat Springs, which gives visitors a short quarter-mile hike to a lower viewpoint. Those wanting a bit of sweat can take the trail to Upper Fish Creek Falls and Long Lake, giving you viewpoints of the area. Depending on the time of the year that you're visiting, you'll see either clear waterfalls or ice in the winter. Open year-round, a $5 private-vehicle daily fee can be paid at the park entrance at 34165 Fish Creek Falls Rd.[40]

Hahns Peak/Bears Ears Ranger District

925 Weiss Dr, Steamboat Springs, CO 80487

970-870-2299

# 13. Dinosaur National Monument

## CENTRAL COLORADO

Dinosaur National Monument represents some of the most significant fossil beds in North America and is located in the southeast section of the Uinta Mountains, bordering Colorado and Utah. The first dinosaur skeleton was discovered in the area by Paleontologist

Earl Douglass of the Carnegie Museum in 1909. This national monument is a paleontologist's dream with a rock layer containing fossils from the Jurassic Period 150 million years ago!

After exploring the fossils, be sure to hike one of the trails, most of which start at the visitors' center. The deep canyons, high mountains, wide rivers, and deserts offer abundant wildlife and landscapes. Fossil Discovery Trail is perfect for families with an easy roundtrip of 2.5 miles. On this trail, kids and adults alike will enjoy touching real dinosaur bones! Of course, for those more adventure-spirited, there are plenty of multi-day rafting outfitters.

Note that the Dinosaur Quarry is located in Utah but well worth the side-trip as it displays over 1,600 bones protruding from a wall of rock. There is no entrance fee to the Quarry exhibit. Also, don't forget to check out the Canyon area (~30 mi. east of Denver) on the Colorado side for spectacular views. Be mindful of its closure during the snow season, which may last until late spring. For camping, check out either the Green River or Yampa River for campgrounds.[29]

Dinosaur National Monument (Utah side)

www.nps.gov

1625 E 1500 S, Jensen, UT 84035

970-374-3000

Dinosaur National Monument (Colorado side)

www.nps.gov

4545 US 40, Dinosaur, CO 81610

*Open 8:00am–5:00pm May–Sep, 9:00am–5:00pm Sep–May.*

*One-Week Pass: $20 per private vehicle*

Getting There & Away: The monument is 88 miles west of Craig via U.S. 40 and 120 miles east of Salt Lake City, UT, by I-80 and U.S. 40. Dinosaur Quarry is 7 miles north of Jensen, UT, on Cub Creek Rd. (Utah Hwy. 149). Monument headquarters is just off U.S. 40 on Harpers Corner Dr., about 4 miles east of the town of Dinosaur.

# 14. Denver

## CENTRAL COLORADO

While many people fly into Denver as a gateway to the Rocky Mountains or any of the other outdoor beauties that exist in Colorado, we recommend a few days to take in what the "mile-high city" has to offer. Sports fans can catch one of their professional sports teams in basketball, baseball, football, soccer, lacrosse, hockey, or rugby. Coors Field or Pepsi Stadium are beautiful venues to grab a beer with thousands of screaming fans. Foodies won't be disappointed as neighborhoods like Rino/Five Points, Highlands, Uptown, or Downtown are lined with great restaurants and breweries. Culture and arts options abound, and we recommend starting with the Public Art Walking Tour to get your bearings on the city. Regardless of the type of traveler you are, Denver has something to offer!

# 15. Public Art Walking Tour in Denver

## CENTRAL COLORADO

*Great art isn't just in museums in Denver. All over the city, you'll find gorgeous murals, whimsical sculptures and other kinds of public art that will delight and inspire. –Denver.org*

Denver's Public Art Program has invested a large amount of money into including public art throughout the city, installing over 150 works throughout downtown and the Golden Triangle Creative Tour. The best way to take in the Denver Art Museum, Denver Public Library, Civic Center Park, Colorado Convention Center, the 16th Street Mall, and the Denver Performing Arts Complex is by foot on a walking tour or bike.[9]

Those interested in street art can check out the Denver Graffiti Tour, a two-hour leisurely walk that starts at 2314 N. Broadway every Saturday (10:00am/11:00am/3:00pm) and Sunday (10:00am).

. . .

https://www.denvergraffititour.com/

info@ denvergraffititour.com

(719) 491-4949

# 16. Denver Art Museum

## CENTRAL COLORADO

The Denver Art Museum (DAM) is located downtown in Denver's Golden Triangle neighborhood. Housing over 70,000 diverse works from across centuries and the world, it is one of the largest art museums in the nation. The museum is known for its collection of

American Indian Art and The Petrie Institute of Western American Art.

Scattered throughout the 8-story museum's more than 200,000 square feet are nine curatorial departments that include the following collections: African Art; Architecture and Design; Art of the Ancient Americas; Asian Art; Modern and Contemporary; Native Arts (African, American Indian, and Oceanic); New World (pre-Columbian and Spanish Colonial); Painting and Sculpture (European and American); Photography; Western American Art; and Textile Art and Fashion.[10]

Several times throughout the year, the DAM offers free general admission through their Free Days at the DAM program. Admission is free to all youth under the age of 18.

denverartmuseum.org

100 W 14th Ave Pkwy, Denver, CO 80204

720-865-5000

*Admission: Non-Resident Adults $13 / Non-Resident Seniors (65+) & College Students $10 / Colorado Resident Adults $10 / Resident Seniors (65+) & College Students $8*

# 17. Museum of Contemporary Art Denver

## CENTRAL COLORADO

Founded in 1996, the Museum of Contemporary Art is the first dedicated home for contemporary art in Denver. Unlike other museums, MCA does not have a permanent collection. The exhibitions are on view for 2–4 months and are rotated about 3–4 times a year.

Aside from arts and exhibits, the museum has a cafe, gift shop, and bar. They also rent out the MCA Cafe for seated dinners, networking events, and cocktail receptions.[1]

To get to the museum, exit at Speer Blvd. (south) from I-25. Merge onto Speer Blvd. going south (toward downtown). Turn left onto Wewatta St. Turn left onto 15th St. Take 15th St. to Delgany St.

MCA Denver is a 4-story dark-gray glass building on the northwest corner of 15th and Delgany.

www.mcadenver.org

1485 Delgany St, Denver, CO 80202

303-298-7554

*Admission: Members Free / Adults $10 / Seniors 65+ $7 / Teachers & College Students (w/ ID) $7 / Teens (13–18) Always Free (under-written by an anonymous donor) / Children (12 and under) Always Free*

*Penny Saturdays: Penny admission on the first Saturday of the month*

# 18. Denver Botanic Gardens

## CENTRAL COLORADO

Labeled as one of the top five botanic gardens in the nation, Denver Botanic Gardens has four locations—each location has its own distinguishing feature.

. . .

The main location, or the formal garden, is located on York St. in Denver. The 24-acre park has a wide range of plants and flowers from all over the world. Inside, you'll also find a cactus and succulent house, a science pyramid exhibition, the Freyer-Newman Center art galleries, the Mordecai Children's Garden, and The Helen Fowler Library.[12]

https://www.botanicgardens.org/york-street

1007 York St, Denver, CO 80206

720-865-3500

*Admission: Members Free / Adults $15 / Seniors (65+) & Military (w/ ID) $11.50 / Children (3–15) & Students (w/ ID) $11 / Children (2 and under) Free*

Chatfield Farms, located in Littleton, is a 700-acre native plant refuge and working farm. The garden has 2.5 miles of nature trails and wildflower gardens. You'll also find the Earl J. Sinnamon Visitor Center; the historical Hildebrand Ranch, a restored 1918 dairy barn and silo; and the 1874 Deer Creek Schoolhouse.[13]

https://www.botanicgardens.org/chatfield-farms

8500 W Deer Creek Canyon Rd, Littleton, CO 80128

720-865-3500

*Hours: 9:00am–4:00pm*

*Admission: Members Free / Adults $10 / Seniors (65+) & Military & Veterans (w/ ID) $7 / Children (3–15) & Students (w/ ID) $7 /*

*Children (2 and under) Free*

The third location is in Hampden Ave. in Aurora. The Plains Conservation Center shares information about the prairie ecosystem and the cultural history of Colorado.[14]

• • •

https://www.botanicgardens.org/other-locations/plains-conservation-center

21901 E. Hampden Ave, Aurora, CO 80013

303-326-8380

Lastly, Mount Goliath is located within the Arapaho National Forest which is the highest cultivated garden in the U.S. There's a timed-entry reservation system to visit Mount Goliath. Visitors can explore the garden, hike the M. Walter Pesman Trail, and visit Dos Chappell Nature Center.[15]

Arapaho National Forest

https://www.botanicgardens.org/other-locations/mount-goliath

Mount Evans Rd, Evergreen, CO 80439

*Mount Goliath and Summit Interpretive Area Vehicle Ticket Rates: 3-Day Personal Vehicle $10*

# 19. Aspen

## CENTRAL COLORADO

Named Aspen due to the abundance of aspen trees in the area, the city is now famed for its ski resorts, the Aspen Music Festival and School, the Aspen Institute, and the Aspen Center for Physics. If you only have a day to spend in the city, make sure to visit Maroon

Bells (see Maroon Bells section), Independence Pass, Aspen Mountain, and the Rio Grande Trail. Wind down at one of the downtown bakeries while enjoying the Dancing Fountain. Shoppers will enjoy downtown with luxury brands such as Gucci and Prada. Note that Aspen isn't for budget travelers and is the most expensive ski town in the U.S.[17]

No matter what kind of activities you fancy, Aspen has a lot to offer. If you plan to visit from December to April, enjoy the mountain winter by downhill skiing or snowboard lessons. Summer months provide rafting, hiking, biking, rock-climbing, fishing, golf, horseback riding, hot-air ballooning, and paragliding.[18]

It's worth noting that aside from the outdoor activities, Aspen has several festivals and events throughout the year: X Games in late January, Jazz Aspen Snowmass, Aspen Music Festival, and Food & Wine Classic.[19]

The easiest way to get to Aspen is via Aspen/Pitkin County Airport (ASE), only 3 miles from downtown Aspen. Other airport options are Eagle County Regional Airport (EGE), Denver International Airport (DEN), and Grand Junction Airport (GJT).[20] [21]

If you're driving from Denver, Travel via I-70 West to Glenwood Springs, then exit Hwy. 82 to Aspen. In the summer months, you can travel to Aspen via Independence Pass. From Denver, take I-70 West to State Hwy. 91 South through Leadville to U.S. 24 South, then west onto Hwy. 82 over Independence Pass. If you'll take

Grand Junction, drive east on I-70 connecting with State Hwy. 82 in Glenwood Springs. Another option is taking the Eagle/Vail route, traveling I-70 West to Glenwood Springs then onto Hwy. 82.

Aspen Chamber Resort Association

https://aspenchamber.org

590 N. Mill St, Aspen, CO 81611

970-925-1940

# 20. Hiking Colorado's Fourteeners

## CENTRAL COLORADO

*"Colorado has 58 mountain peaks exceeding 14,000 feet (known as "fourteeners" or "14ers" locally)—the most of any state."*
*–Colorado.com*

. . .

While many visitors may not know the difference or be able to identify them, the 14ers are the main draw for hardcore mountaineers. The most famous include Pikes Peak, Maroon Bells, Mount Crested Butte, Longs Peak, and Mount Evans. When visiting any of these mountains, be mindful of the altitude. If you aren't up for the task of climbing up to 14,000 feet above sea level, many mountains have campgrounds at the base, which provide splendid hikes through meadows.

## 21. Maroon Bells

### CENTRAL COLORADO

North of Aspen is home to the Maroon Bells, two of the most photographed mountains in the nation. Located in the Elk Mountain range, it is no surprise how famous the Maroon Peak and North Maroon Peak are. Maroon Lake is the best spot to take it all in, with its fresh water providing a mirror-like reflection of the mountains and Aspen trees along the valley.

•••

Nature enthusiasts will not be disappointed as there are many hiking trails, campsites, and biking paths. July surrounds visitors with beautiful alpine meadows displaying wildflowers in full bloom. September has cooler fall weather, with the Aspen trees turning amber yellow. Regardless of when you visit, you will see road cyclists going up Maroon Creek Rd. We recommend starting your trip at the Maroon Bells Basecamp to get oriented about the National Forest Service campgrounds that scatter the area and trail information.[22] [23]

Aspen-Sporis Ranger District

https://aspenchamber.org/plan-trip/trip-highlights/maroon-bells/reservations

620 Main St, Carbondale, CO 81623

970-930-6442

*Open from June and October*

*Reservations are required to access the Maroon Bells Scenic Area and related amenities by vehicle or by RFTA shuttle. As of 2021, the price of a parking reservation is $10 per vehicle.*

*Advance Purchase Round-Trip Shuttle Tickets: Adults $16 / Seniors (65+) $10 / Children (under 12) $10*

# 22. Vail

## CENTRAL COLORADO

Vail is a small town at the base of Vail Mountain and is home to the 5,000+ acre Vail Ski Resort. Whether you are traveling during summer or winter, there are many outdoor activities to enjoy in the area. Most notable in the summer is the Shrine Pass, with its multiuse trail that allows for biking, hiking, or driving an ATV. It becomes the Vail Pass Recreation Area hosting snowmobilers, backcountry skiers, and snowboarders in the winter. Other recommended areas are the Vail Nature Center and Epic Discovery during the summer; Vail Mountain and Adventure Ridge in winter. Alpine Quest Sports will be your go-to outfitter for kayaking adventures. Vail Golf Club is an excellent 18-hole, par 71 haven located 8,200 feet above sea level.

Vail Nature Center

www.walkingmountains.org

601 Vail Valley Dr, Vail, CO 81657

970-479-2291

*The Vail Nature Center is a free-admission learning center.*

Take a break from the action-packed activities and pay a visit to the Colorado Ski Museum to learn about the history of skiing. Plant lovers will enjoy the Betty Ford Alpine Gardens, which hosts a wide range of native alpine plants and Himalayan-collected species. There are plenty of restaurants in the area, including the world-renowned establishments The Tenth and Game Creek Restaurant. If you get your timing right, Vail also holds several festivals, parties, and events. There's a party to close the ski season, the Taste of Vail and the Vail Film Festival in April. Snow Daze calls itself "the largest early-season mountain bash in North America." Vail is the ultimate adult playground!

. . .

Betty Ford Alpine Gardens

bettyfordalpinegardens.org

522 S Frontage Rd E, Vail, CO 81657

970-476-0103

*Admission: There is no required admission fee, however a $5 donation per person is suggested.*

Getting to Vail:

From Denver International Airport (DIA), take Peña Blvd. to I-70 W, then take exit 176 for Vail. From Eagle/Vail Airport (EGE), take Cooley Mesa Rd. (main airport road) to Hwy. 6. Take a right on Hwy. 6. Follow Hwy. 6 to signs for I-70 East and drive for 25–30 minutes and take exit 176 for Vail. It's important to note that it's easy to get around Vail using public transportation. You can use a bike, their free transport, or just walk around![27]

Vail, CO

www.vailgov.com

# 23. Booth Falls Trail

## CENTRAL COLORADO

The Booth Falls Trail is one of the most popular hikes in the Eagles Nest Wilderness. The trail is 4.5 miles long, with views of the peaks of the Gore Range, rivers, valleys, and aspen grove forests. The path is primarily used for hiking and nature trips and is best used from May until October.

• • •

From Booth Falls, you can head straight to Booth Lake. The lake at the top of the mountain is impressive. The hike is rated difficult, and the last 1/4 mile to Booth Lake is steep and rocky.

Getting to the trailhead is easy. You can take the free bus from the Vail Transportation Center. The free East Vail blue line shuttle runs every 30 minutes from the Vail Transportation Center to the Booth Falls stop. Walk up Booth Falls Rd. a 1/4 mile to the trailhead. The parking closure is a pilot program to address the negative impacts of overcrowding on the Eagles Nest Wilderness, such as a buildup of waste, trail erosion, and other safety concerns (speeding, illegal parking, emergency vehicle access, etc.) that impact nearby residents and guests as well.[28]

www.fs.usda.gov

3035 Booth Falls Rd, Vail, CO 81657

# 24. Mount Evans

## CENTRAL COLORADO

To reach the summit of Mount Evans, you have to traverse Colorado's highest byway which also happens to be the highest paved road in North America. The Mount Evans Scenic Byway consists of State Hwy. 103 from Idaho Springs, Colorado on I-70 about 13 miles to Echo Lake, and Colorado 5 from Echo Lake 15 miles, ending at a parking area and turnaround just below the summit. A reminder that the byway is only open during summer when the conditions are safe for driving.[61]

• • •

Driving through the mountainside will give you views of the valleys and the rocky peaks. You may also see mountain goats, marmots, and bighorn sheep while driving up or down the byway. Once at the apex, the views will stretch across the entire Front Range, including a spectacular shot at 14,110-foot Pikes Peak to the south.

Mt. Evans Welcome Center

www.fs.usda.gov

16 Mount Evans Hwy, Idaho Springs, CO 80452

303-567-3000

*In order to access the Mount Evans Scenic Byway, you will need to pay a $15 fee (vehicles carrying more than 12 passengers will be required to pay more). Hikers, bikers, Federal Recreation Passport holders, and those who simply drive to the top and back without stopping will not have to pay.*

# 25. Argo Mill and Tunnel

## CENTRAL COLORADO

The Argo Mill and Tunnel is an intact gold mill located in Idaho Springs, Colorado. As one of the most significant milling operations in the world, the area provides a great introduction to the gold rush of Colorado and the working conditions of the times. An educational tour explains how the mine processed over one hundred million dollars' worth of gold ore.

. . .

Open year-round, this site is an excellent place for history buffs and families. Visitors are briefed with a historical movie then given a mining equipment demo, a tunnel tour, and then a descent into the mill structure. In addition, there is an indoor museum that displays mining artifacts. Visitors will also learn how to pan for gold.[62]

www.argomilltour.com

2350 Riverside Dr, Idaho Springs, CO 80452

303-567-2421

*Open 7 days a week 10:00am–6:00pm*

*Admission: Adults $25*

# 26. Glenwood Springs

## CENTRAL COLORADO

Commonly referred to as "Up Valley," Glenwood Springs is known for its thermal hot springs and outdoor adventures. Located an hour away from other fantastic ski destinations, Vail and Aspen, it offers excellent skiing at an affordable price. Sunlight Mountain Resort is an excellent space for ability levels in cross-country skiing, snow-shoeing, and ice-skating.

. . .

● ● ●

One of the more famous attractions in the area is Glenwood Caverns Adventure Park which sits at an altitude of 7,100 feet on a mountain above Glenwood. They have a tram ride that will take you to the top of the Iron Mountain, the Historic Fairy Cave and King's Row tour, and an amusement park.

A trip to Glenwood Springs wouldn't be complete without a visit to the hot springs. Glenwood Hot Springs & Spa of the Rockies is a 125-year-old resort with great amenities, including water slides, spa, and mini-golf. Head over to Yampah Spa if you want heat, which gives off an extremely hot (110°F) inside temperature.

Glenwood Hot Springs Pool

www.hotspringspool.com

401 N River St, Glenwood Springs, CO 81601

970-947-2955

*Check https://www.hotspringspool.com/pool/rates#rates-individual for rates.*

Yampah Spa

https:// yampahspa.com/contact/

709 E. Sixth St. Glenwood Springs, CO 81601

970-945-0667

*Check https://yampahspa.com/menu/ for rates and services.*

Glenwood Springs is served by four airports. Eagle/Vail is 30 miles east, Aspen is 40 miles south, Grand Junction is 90 miles west, and Denver International Airport is 180 miles east of Glenwood Springs. There is the option to fly into one of two non-commercial airports: Glenwood Springs Municipal Airport (GWS).[45]

Glenwood Springs, CO

www.ci.glenwood-springs.co.us

Glenwood Caverns Adventure Park

www.glenwoodcaverns.com

51000 Two Rivers Plaza Rd, Glenwood Springs, CO 81601

970-945-4228

*Tickets: Gondola $21 / Gondola & Caves $34 / Gondola, Caves & Rides FUNDAY $61*

# 27. Breckenridge

## CENTRAL COLORADO

A Colorado town set at the base of the Rocky Mountains' Tenmile Range, Breckenridge is known for its Gold Rush history, ski resort, and year-round alpine activities. To learn about the history of Breckenridge, visit Barney Ford Museum, Boreas Pass, Lomax

Placer Mine, and the Summit Ski Museum. Breckenridge Arts District has plenty of galleries, performance spaces, and an exhibition hall if you're into the arts.

For snow sports enthusiasts, the Breckenridge Ski Area has the best beginner and intermediate terrain in the state. The Breckenridge Nordic Center manages nine cross-country trails and five snowshoe trails. In the summer, you can hike through the McCullough Gulch trail, and it'll lead you to thundering falls and a glacial lake. Mountain bikers of all levels have space on hundreds of miles of off-road biking and scenic paved paths. Those preferring ice should spend time at the Stephen C. West Ice Arena, home to indoor and outdoor ice rinks.

Just like Aspen and Vail, Breckenridge likes to throw parties. The Breckenridge Music Festival is celebrated every summer and winter, the International Snow Sculpture Championship is a three-week event starting in mid-January, and Mardi Gras falls in February. Bikers will enjoy Breck Bike Week each June, which includes a skills clinic and displays of demo gear.[30]

Breckenridge, CO

www.townofbreckenridge.com

Getting to Breckenridge is easy: a mere 80 miles west of Denver via I-70 take exit 203, then Hwy. 9 south. Guests mostly fly out to Denver International Airport (DEN). Instead of driving, most guests take an airport shuttle to Breckenridge. Transportation won't be a problem while in town as most of the hotels offer a free shuttle and the town offers a free bus system.[31]


Breckenridge Tourism Office

https://gobreck.com/

203 S. Main Street Breckenridge, CO 80424

970-453-2913

# 28. Browns Canyon National Monument

## CENTRAL COLORADO

On February 19, 2015, President Barack Obama designated the space of more than 21,000 acres of canyons, rivers, and forest as Browns Canyon National Monument. The pristine area is home to black bears, elk, bighorn sheep, falcons, and eagles, making it a popular wildlife viewing park. Most visitors come to the rugged terrain searching for an adrenaline rush on the Class IV and V whitewater rafting rapids of the Arkansas River. Beyond that, recreationists will enjoy mountain biking, horseback riding, hiking, nature photography, and stargazing. Anglers won't be disappointed as the river is named a world-class area for wild trout fishing. On your way in (or out), don't forget a stop at Buena Vista or Salida, both great artsy towns near the national monument.[46] [47]

Salida, CO

www.blm.gov

Browns Canyon National Monument

https://www.blm.gov/programs/national-conservation-lands/colorado/browns-canyon

3028 E Main St, Canon City, CO 81212

719-269-8500

*Browns Canyon National Monument does not require fees for entrance. However, parking at the Ruby Mountain Recreation Area Site and/or the Hecla Junction Recreation Site requires either a Colorado Parks and Wildlife annual or daily parks pass. Annual parks passes may be obtained at the Arkansas Headwaters Visitor Center in Salida, Colorado or daily passes can be obtained at self-serve kiosks at the recreation sites.*

# 29. Florissant Fossil Bed National Monument

## CENTRAL COLORADO

Located in central Colorado, the Florissant Fossil Beds National Monument is a beautiful mountain valley filled with the world's richest, most diverse fossil deposits. As an ancient lake deposit and former Sequoia forest, petrified redwood stumps as wide as 14 feet scatter the area and provide insight into prehistoric Colorado.[6]

• • •

*Florissant Fossil Beds National Monument has yielded over 50,000 museum specimens from fossils of over 1,700 species: 1,500 insects, 150 plants, and one of the world's only known fossil records of the tsetse fly, now found only in equatorial Africa. This world-class snapshot records Eocene Epoch life here 34 million years ago. –NPS History eLibrary*

If you want to dig for your own fossils, visit the Florissant Fossil Quarry, next door to the national monument. Beyond fossil beds, spend an evening with volunteers from the Colorado Springs Astronomical Society as they host night sky programs open to the public.

Florissant Fossil Quarry

https://www.florissantfossilquarry.com/

18117 Teller County Rd 1, Florissant, CO 80816

719-748-3275

*Hours: 10:00am–5:00pm 7 days a week from Memorial Day through Labor Day.*[6]

# 30. Mesa Verde National Park

## SOUTHWEST COLORADO

The mysterious Mesa Verde National Park was established in 1906 to preserve and interpret 600 ancient cliff dwellings left by Ancestral Puebloans in the 1300s. For adventurers, the 81 square miles of park are full of carved-out dwellings with rock art depicting scenes of ancient America.

. . .

Our recommendation for seeing the area is through an hour-long tour led by park rangers. They will help you crawl through tunnels, climb ladders, and give you a lay of the land, along with some theories on why the ancient civilization disappeared. Anthropologists will want to stay a bit longer as Mesa Verde has done a fabulous job of maintaining the cultural heritage of the Puebloans, giving much to explore.[16]

If you plan to spend more than a day in the park, Mesa Verde National Park hosts a campsite and lodges (open only during certain months). Keep in mind that you need a ranger to continue in some areas, while in other areas, you require a ticket. Throughout the park, restrooms, food service, and picnic services are accessible. There are several bicycle paths. Don't forget to wear sunscreen and pack extra water. Also, don't miss Cliff Palace: with 150 rooms it is North America's largest cliff dwelling.

www.visitmesaverde.com

Mesa Verde National Park, CO 81330

970-529-4465

*The park is always open, except under emergency conditions. Sites, trails, and picnic areas are open 8:00am–sunset.*

*Admission: The entrance fee for the park is $20 per car from May 1–October 31 and $15 per car for the rest of the year. Ranger-led walking tours of Cliff Palace, Balcony House, and Long House are available on varying schedules; admission ticket purchase is required for a nominal fee.*

# 31. Silverton

## SOUTHWEST COLORADO

Surrounded by white-capped peaks and old western mining tales, the small town of Silverton (population 630) gives visitors great insight into what pioneers experienced during the silver rush. This Colorado playground transports visitors by steam train in the summer and by snowmobiles in the winter.

. . .

. . .

The scenery is best taken in through the Durango and Silverton Narrow Gauge Railroad (see the separate section on Durango). It is a must for visitors as it is regularly named the best scenic train ride in the nation. Note the trip from Ouray to Silverton takes you along the Million Dollar Highway and is easily one of the state's most epic road trips. Regardless of your mode of transportation in and around Silverton, the natural beauty will be ever-present.

History buffs will enjoy the Mining Heritage Center (open June–October, costing $8 for adults, $3 per child). The museum is outfitted with rustic mining equipment and hosts a blacksmith shop.

Mining Heritage Center

www.sanjuancountyhistoricalsociety.org

1557 Greene St, Courthouse Square, Silverton, CO 81433

970-387-5609

Whether going extreme with heli-skiing, riding snowmobiles, or relaxing on hiking trails, those seeking adventure won't be disappointed. Silverton Mountain Ski area receives over 400 inches of snowfall each year; advanced skiers can go on guided ski runs with locals. In March and April, unguided day tickets are also given. For the more advanced, there's a 6 Run Heli Day which drops skiers in exclusive terrain.[25]

For beginners and families check out Kendall Mountain Recreation Area where skis, sleds, and tubes can be rented.


• • •


Kendall Mountain Recreation Area

www.skikendall.com

1 Kendall Pl, Silverton, CO 81433

970-387-5522


Silverton Mountain Ski Area

www.silvertonmountain.com

6226 State Hwy 110, Silverton, CO 81433

970-387-5706

# 32. Black Canyon of the Gunnison National Park

## SOUTHWEST COLORADO

The Black Canyon of the Gunnison is described as one of the deepest, narrowest, and longest canyons in North America. Its name reflects the sparse 33 minutes of daily sunlight some of the narrowest parts receive. The surrounding area is an outdoor paradise, with the Gunnison River being known for its fishing territory that includes brown and rainbow trout and Kokanee salmon.

• • •

To reach the Gunnison River during summer, it is recommended to take East Portal Rd. Another option is to take South Rim Rd. which follows a path near the canyon rim which gives travelers 11 viewpoints. Those wanting to spend more time in the area hike the 7-mile round trip North Vista Trail. If you make it to Exclamation Point, you'll find several beautiful inner-canyon views.

The park can be accessed with a private vehicle. Black Canyon's South Rim is about 14 miles from Montrose and 63 miles from Gunnison. To get there from Montrose, travel 7 miles north on CO Hwy. 347 from the intersection with U.S. Hwy. 50 east of the city.[36][37]

Black Canyon of the Gunnison National Park

https://www.nps.gov/blca/index.htm

9800 Highway 347 Montrose, CO 81401

970-641-2337 x205

• • •

*The park is open 24 hours a day, every day, and no entry reservation is needed.*

*Entrance Fee: Per Vehicle $30*

*Covers all persons in a single, private, noncommercial vehicle and is valid for seven calendar days.*

*Entrance Fee: Per Motorcycle $25*

*Covers up to two people on a single motorcycle and is valid for seven calendar days.*

# 33. Durango

## SOUTHWEST COLORADO

Durango is a town in southwest Colorado that dates its origins to the 1880s during the U.S. rail transportation system boom. These systems were brought in to transport silver and other commodities and provide for the expansion of the nation into the west, connecting the interior of the U.S. to the Pacific Ocean.[26] The city center is home to the Railroad Museum, which displays many restored locomotives.

In addition, the Powerhouse Science Center is an interactive science center perfect for families and adults, centered around energy-related themes.

Powerhouse Science Center

https://powsci.org

info@powsci.org

1333 Camino del Rio, Durango, CO 81301

970-259-9234

*Admission: Members Free / Adults $14 / Seniors, Military & Student $10 / Children (3–17) $10 / Children (2 and under) FREE*

While mentioned in our Silverton section, the Durango & Silverton Narrow Gauge Railroad is a family-friendly must-do as it traverses the gorgeous backcountry of Colorado. Durango provides a great jumping-off point for exploring the remote wilderness and high mountains of the San Juan National Forest.

Durango Area Tourism Office

www.durangogov.org

802 Main Ave, Durango, CO 81301

970-247-3500

# 34. San Juan National Forest

## SOUTHWEST COLORADO

The San Juan National Forest is 3,000 square miles of federal lands with terrain ranging from high-desert mesas to alpine peaks filled with back roads and trails for exploring. The area features the San Juan Skyway, a Bureau of Land Management 4WD scenic byway, the Alpine Loop Backcountry Byway, and a National Forest scenic byway. The forest encompasses three wilderness areas: Weminuche Wilderness, South San Juan Wilderness, and Lizard Head Wilderness—two of which are alpine wilderness areas.[54]

You'll never run out of areas to explore with an abundance of hiking trails and campgrounds. Aside from hiking, you can go boating, cross-country skiing, or horseback riding. The Lower Animas River has turbulent water and has the nickname "River of Lost Souls," which is excellent for rafting and kayaking. There's Pine River, Weminuche Creek, and several lakes perfect for fishing. You can also drive along the San Juan Skyway, a 233-mile loop carving through the mountain range.

https://www.fs.usda.gov/detail/sanjuan/about-forest/districts/?cid=stelprdb5154743

15 Burnett Court Durango, CO 81301

970-247-4874

# 35. The Million Dollar Highway, San Juan Skyway

## SOUTHWEST COLORADO

The Million Dollar Highway is one of the most picturesque drives in the country. According to stories, the highway got its name because it cost a million dollars a mile to build it, while other legends state that its fill-dirt contains a million dollars in gold ore.

. . .

• • •

Though the entire stretch has been called the Million Dollar Highway, it is really the 12 miles south of Ouray through the Uncompahgre Gorge to the summit of Red Mountain Pass, which gains the highway its name. It is part of the San Juan Skyway. This stretch through the gorge is challenging and potentially hazardous to drive; it is characterized by steep cliffs, narrow lanes, and a lack of guardrails. The ascent of Red Mountain Pass is marked with some hairpin curves used to gain elevation, and again, narrow lanes for traffic—many cut directly into the sides of mountains.[55]

While driving this road, it's also important to remember that there aren't any guardrails or shoulders—so take extra caution! The weather in this zone is highly unpredictable and may change from sunny to moderate or heavy snowfall quickly. Avalanches, snowfalls, and landslides can also occur anytime. At times, it causes roadblocks which makes it hazardous.

Million Dollar Highway, US-550, Silverton, CO 81433

# 36. Telluride

## SOUTHWEST COLORADO

ONCE A FORMER SILVER MINING CAMP, Telluride

is now known as Colorado's most remote ski destination. Surrounded by alpine scenery, skiers will most certainly enjoy the steep and deep terrain of the Telluride Ski Resort. Although the terrain is recommended for advanced and intermediate skiers, beginners will still enjoy the area. The resort also offers private and group lessons if you'd like to enhance your skills.

Telluride Ski Resort

Mountain Village Center, 565 Mountain Village Blvd, Telluride, CO 81435

1 800-778-8581

*Hours: 9:00am–4:30pm*

The Smithsonian-affiliated Telluride Historical Museum (opened year-round) showcases the region's geologic history and mining history. There are plenty of all-season trail rides for horseback riding in the surrounding hills. For adventure sports, Telluride Mountain Guides offers backcountry skiing, mountaineering, hiking, rock and ice climbing with experienced guides. Telluride Outside will help you whether you want to go fly fishing, mountain-bike tours, 4WD tours, or rafting.

Telluride Historical Museum

201 W. Gregory Ave (at the top of Fir St), Telluride, CO 81435

970-728-3344

*Hours: Mondays to Saturdays from 11:00am–5:00pm / Thursdays open until 7:00pm*

*Admission Fees: General Admission $7 / Seniors (65+) $5 / Students (6–17) $5*

. . .

• • •

Events are plentiful, so be sure to check out Telluride's official website. In May, the Mountainfilm documentary film festival screens outdoor adventure and environmental films over four days. Telluride has a packed festival schedule in the summer, including the Hot Air Balloon Festival, which traditionally occurs the first weekend in June. June also hosts the Telluride Bluegrass Festival, an annual music fest. Every September is the Telluride Film Festival, a Labor Day weekend film festival.

https://www.telluride.com/ play/festivals-events/

During ski season, there are flights to Montrose Regional Airport to reach Telluride. Depending on the weather, there are also commuter flights to Telluride airport. Due to its boxed location, there's only one way to drive to town. There are available shuttles and bus routes that can take you downtown and to nearby communities.

Telluride, CO

www.telluride-co.gov

# 37. Colorado National Monument

## SOUTHWEST COLORADO

The Colorado National Monument shadows the city of Grand Junction and is home to red-rock formations in the desert highlands of Western Colorado. With its temperate semi-arid climate, it is home to various wildlife, including golden eagles, desert bighorn sheep, coyotes, and red-tailed hawks. Those pressed for time can opt for a scenic drive or slow the pace down on a bicycle or horseback riding through the countryside. Hiking is bountiful, with scenic viewpoints at Rim Rock Dr. A side trip here would include a visit to Book Cliffs, a shared flat-topped mountain on the border of Eastern Utah and Western Colorado.

www.nps.gov

Rimrock Dr, Fruita, CO 81521

970-858-3617

https://www.nps.gov/colm/planyourvisit/basicinfo.htm

1750 Rim Rock Dr, Fruita, CO 81521

970-858-2800

*Hours: The Monument is open 24 hours a day year-round. Rim Rock Rd. is only closed for poor road conditions (snow, ice, rock fall, etc.).*

*Entrance Fees: Private, non-commercial vehicle $25 / Motorcycle $20 / Individual (hiker, bicyclist) $15*

# 38. Colorado Springs

## SOUTHEAST COLORADO

COLORADO SPRINGS, at an elevation of 6,035 ft., is a city in Colorado with a wide-open landscape at the eastern foot of the Rocky Mountains and is blessed with natural landscapes. Culture, art, entertainment, and interesting history are embedded in the town of Colorado Springs. There is an abundance of family activities, from hiking trails to rafting or ziplining. This playground is perfect for couples, families, or solo travelers. For adventure, head to the Broadmoor Manitou or hop on the Pikes Peak Cog Railway (read more in the Pikes Peak & Garden of the Gods section). Once you get off the train, visit the Summit Visitor Center on Pikes Peak, also named America's Mountain. This will be your jump-off point for outdoor adventure.[6]

For itineraries in and around Pikes Peak check out their official tourism website at https://www.pikes-peak.com/.

Colorado Springs Visitor Information Center

https://www.visitcos.com/

515 S Cascade Ave, Colorado Springs, CO 80903719-635-7506 or 1 800-888-4748

# 39. Colorado Springs Fine Arts Center

## SOUTHEAST COLORADO

The Colorado Springs Fine Arts Center at Colorado College (FAC) is located just north of downtown Colorado Springs, Colorado. The Center is home to world-class art galleries, Broadway-worthy live theatre, and an art school for the young and old.

. . .

• • •

The Fine Arts Center's museum collection features many master-works from top Modern American artists, including Richard Diebenkorn, Georgia O'Keeffe, Walt Kuhn, John Singer Sargent, Dale Chihuly, and artists connected to the renowned Broadmoor Art Academy. The Fine Arts Center also has one of the most substantial Hispanic, Latin American, and Native American collections in the nation. If you get hungry, drop into the restaurant, Taste, which has a fantastic view of Pikes Peak.[8]

fac.coloradocollege.edu

30 W Dale St, Colorado Springs, CO 80903

719-634-5581

*General Museum Admission: FAC Members Free / Non-member Adults $10 / Military & Seniors (55+) (w/ ID) $5 / Students & Teachers (w/ ID) Free*

Directions to the Fine Arts Center from I-25: Take exit 143, Uintah St.

Go east on Uintah to Cascade Ave. Turn right onto Cascade Ave.

Go south on Cascade to Dale St.

Turn right onto Dale St, the Fine Arts Center is on the right (the only building on the block).

# 40. Sangre de Cristo Mountains

## SOUTHEAST COLORADO

Spanish for "blood of Christ," the Sangre de Cristo Mountains are the southernmost subrange of the Rocky Mountains. The mountains run from Poncha Pass in south-central Colorado, trending southeast and south, ending at Glorieta Pass, just southeast of Santa Fe, New

Mexico. The mountains contain many fourteen thousand foot peaks in the Colorado portion. Also located in the Sangres are the San Isabel, Rio Grande, Carson, and Santa Fe National Forests. National Wilderness areas include Sangre de Cristo, Wheeler Peak, Latir Peaks, Pecos, and Spanish Peaks.[64]

There are a lot of activities that you can try out while in the mountains. It's a popular area for camping, cross-country and downhill skiing, rafting, rock climbing, and hiking. There are also hidden spots throughout the mountains that are best for stargazing, fishing, and hunting.

While the mountains are a fascinating place to explore, the towns scattered in and alongside the Sangre de Cristo Mountains provide a fascinating snapshot of the region's contemporary culture as well as an enlightening window far into its past. You'll find adobe pueblo structures that make up the Taos Pueblo, the Blue Lake that sits high atop the range near Wheeler Peak, The High Road to Taos.[65]

https://spanishpeakscountry.com/the-sangre-de-cristo-mountains/

Most of the publicly accessible areas are managed by the United States Forest Service.

Information Centers:

San Carlos Ranger District 719-269-8500

Pike and San Isabel National Forests 719-553-1400

Great Sand Dunes National Park & Preserve 719-378-6395

• • •

To get to Sangre de Cristo Mountains from Denver, get on I-25 S from W. Colfax Ave. then follow I-25 S. to I-25BL S. in Huerfano County. Take exit 52 from I-25 S. toward US-160 W. Follow signs and merge onto I-25BL S. Take US-160 W. and CO-159 S. to County Road J.2 in Costilla County.

To get to Sangre de Cristo Mountains from Colorado Springs, get on I-25 S. from S. Nevada Ave. Follow I-25 S. to I-25BL S. in Huerfano County. Take exit 52 from I-25 S. toward US-160 W. Follow signs and merge onto I-25BL S. Take US-160 W. and CO-159 S to County Road J.2 in Costilla County.

# 41. Pikes Peak & Garden of the Gods

## SOUTHEAST COLORADO

A designated national natural landmark, Garden of the Gods is a public park originally called Red Rock Corral by the Europeans. The garden's ecology is diverse, home to more than 130 species of birds, mule deer, bighorn sheep, fox, and many animals. Activities in the park include hiking, technical rock climbing, road and mountain biking, and horseback riding. Trolley or jeep tours are also available. There is also a Segway Tour which is a fun way to combine history lessons and outdoor activity.[5]

You can view Pikes Peak from the balcony of the Garden of the Gods. The most famous among Colorado's fourteeners, Pikes Peak was once called the Mountain of the Sun. To reach the peak, visitors can take the Pikes Peak Highway, the Broadmoor Manitou and Pikes Peak Cog Railway, or go via the Barr Trail.

Trekking through the Barr Trail usually takes two days to hike the 26-mile out-and-back trail from Manitou Springs to Pikes Peak. This is recommended for experienced backcountry hikers.

Using the Broadmoor Manitou and Pikes Peak Cog Railway, a round-trip ride will take 3 hours and 10 minutes, including 40 minutes at the top. Visitors travel aboard diesel-powered Swiss-built trains, which definitely makes it more interesting.

The Broadmoor Manitou and Pikes Peak Cog Railway

cograilway.com

515 Ruxton Ave, Manitou Springs, CO 80829

719-685-5401

Note that both the Garden of the Gods and Pikes Peak are in Manitou Springs, 6 miles west of Colorado Springs along Hwy. 24.

. . .

. . .

Pike's Peak

https://coloradosprings.gov/pikes-peak-americas-mountain

5089 Pikes Peak Hwy, Cascade, CO 80809

719-385-7325

*America's Mountain is open year-round, weather permitting.*

*Cost: Adults $15 / Child (6-15) $5 / Carload (up to 5 people) $50*


Garden of the Gods

https://www.gardenofgods.com

1805 N. 30th St, Colorado Springs, CO, 80904

719-634-6666

*Park Hours: 5:00am–9:00pm (Nov 1–Apr 30) / 5:00am–10:00pm (May 1–Oct 31)*

*Visitor & Nature Center Hours: 9:00am–5:00pm (Winter months) / 8:00am–5:00pm (Summer, Memorial Day Weekend & Labor Day Weekend)*

*Cost: Both the Park and Visitor & Nature Center are FREE and open to the public.*

# 42. Manitou Springs Incline

## SOUTHEAST COLORADO

The Manitou Springs Incline is a steep 1-mile trail with an elevation gain of 2,000 feet on an intense, uneven staircase. But who doesn't like a challenge, right? This vigorous hike is only recommended for physically active visitors and those already adjusted to the elevation of the mountains. The base of the peak starts at 6,500 feet and the highest point is 8,590 feet.

If going down with wobbly legs isn't for you, note that there is access to the Barr Trail that gives hikers a more gentle descent.

Reservations are required to hike the Manitou Incline and can be made at the Manitou Incline reservation page on the City of Colorado Springs website.[50]

Manitou Incline Reservations

https:// cityofcoloradosprings.aluvii.com/store/shop/productdetails? id=1&productId=1

354 Manitou Ave, Manitou Springs, CO

719-685-5089

*Hours: 6:00am–6:00pm*

*Cost: This incredible hike is free to use. Shuttle #33 gives you a free trip and runs every 20 minutes from 6:00am to 6:00pm daily.*

*Limited paid parking is available at the trailhead near 530 Ruxton Ave.*

*\*Shuttle 33 is a year-round Incline shuttle that services the Incline and downtown. Park at 10 Old Man's Trail, 8082. Free shuttle picks up near the statue at east end of Memorial Park, Manitou.*

# 43. Cave of the Winds Mountain Park

## SOUTHEAST COLORADO

The Cave of the Winds Mountain Park is an outdoor park filled with underground caverns and is a must-see Colorado Springs attraction.

Wedged between Pikes Peak and Manitou Springs, there are three cave tours, appropriate for all ages. Discovered in 1881 by George and John Pickett when the two explored a nearby crevice by candlelight, crawling through a limestone arch into a large chamber that turned out to be an underground network of caves. Regardless of which tour you take, you'll see stalactites, stalagmites, and underground geological features. Beyond the caves, there are several activities for thrill-seekers. There's a rock-climbing wall, ziplines, and a via ferrata.[7]

www.caveofthewinds.com

100 Cave of the Winds Rd, Manitou Springs, CO 80829

719-685-5444

# 44. Alpine Loop

## SOUTHEAST COLORADO

The Alpine Loop is a 65-mile road that connects Lake City, Ouray, and Silverton. The byway also passes through several ghost towns. It's important to note that the Loop is only open when it's snow-free, usually from late May or early June until September or October, and a 4WD high-clearance vehicle is needed to traverse this route.

•  •  •

Activities while in Lake City include hiking, camping, and mountain biking over hundreds of miles of hiking and off-road trails.[51]

Also known as the "Switzerland of America," Ouray earned its nickname because of its climate, natural alpine environment, and scenery. Visitors can also enjoy ice climbing, hiking, and mountain biking while in the city. It has also become a popular destination for motorcyclists, as it marks the beginning of the Million Dollar Highway.[52]

Silverton is located within 15 miles of seven of Colorado's most famous fourteeners, making it one of the premier gateways into the state's deep backcountry. The town has a lot of trails for hiking and mountain biking. There's also the option of camping, horseback riding, and rafting while in the area.[53]

## 45. Royal Gorge

### SOUTHEAST COLORADO

The Royal Gorge is one of the most popular attractions in Colorado, inviting everyone from road-tripping families to thrill-seeking adventurers to explore this beautiful area's canyon, train, rafting, zip lines, and other amusements in the Cañon City area. The Park is most famous for the Royal Gorge Bridge, and is home to what was once the world's highest suspension bridge, until China completed the Beipan River Guanxing Highway Bridge in 2003. It is currently the highest in the U.S. The 360-acre park is excellent for families and is packed with breathtaking views and adrenaline rides, including the Royal Rush Skycoaster and the Cloudscraper Zipline that lets you fly 1,200 feet above the Arkansas River.

royalgorgebridge.com

4218 County Rd 3A, Cañon City, CO 81212

719-275-7507

*For updated hours check https://royalgorgebridge.com/ hours-directions/*

*Visitor Center, Rides, and Attractions open at 10:00am daily.*

From Denver go south on I-25. Take Exit 140 (Tejon St.) toward Cañon City via Hwy. 115 S. On exit ramp, proceed through 1st intersection to 2nd intersection (Nevada Ave.). Turn right on Nevada Ave. which becomes Hwy. 115 S. (approx. 33 miles). Right on Hwy. 50 W. (approx. 15 miles). Left (south) on County Road 3A (approx. 4 miles).[63]

# 46. Skyline Drive

## SOUTHEAST COLORADO

Skyline Drive is an epic 2.6-mile drive on a narrow one-way road on top of a razorback ridge that overlooks the city of Cañon City. At the end of the one-way road, hop off and take the 1-mile out-and-back trek on the Old Skyline Drive Trail for even more spectacular views. Interestingly, the road was built on the backs of 60 inmates from the nearby prison and completed in 1905. Note that this trip combines well with a stay in the Royal Gorge area just 9 miles away.


Cañon City, CO

https://www.colorado.com/scenic-historic-byways/skyline-drive

*Roads: 2WD, one-way*

*Length: 2.6 miles*

*Cost: Free*

*Open: Year-round*

# 47. Great Sand Dunes National Park

## SOUTHEAST COLORADO

Located in southern Colorado, the Great Sand Dunes National Park is known for its high dunes and jagged peaks, with sublime geography consisting of tundra, sand dunes, wetland, and forest. While in the park, it is highly recommended to trek Montville Nature Trail if you want a quick trip or you're with children. Go to Mosca Pass Trail, a moderate 7-mile-round-trip hike, and Zapata Falls if you want to wade through ankle-deep ice-cold water and slippery rocks.

Guests mostly visit the Medano Creek, which flows down from the Sangre de Cristos and the eastern sand dunes. During peak flow, it becomes a temporary beach which is excellent for families. There are two informal hikes in the park—the shorter is High Dune, and the tallest is Star Dune.

Just a reminder, when trekking these dunes, wear sunscreen and closed-toe shoes.

If you're up for a thrilling activity, you won't go wrong with dune sandboarding, sledding, and mountain biking. A 4-mile trail is available in the Zapata Falls Special Recreation Area, but there's also a grueling path going to Medano Pass. If you're into sandboarding, the best time to do it is after precipitation. When it's too dry, you'll just sink. On the flip side, sledding when snow is covering the dunes is excellent. Not equipped? No problem. There are rental shops around the area.

While exploring the park during the day is fun, staying and traversing during nighttime is also a great idea. In 2019, Great Sand Dunes became a certified International Dark Sky Park by the International Dark-Sky Association. This means that the park's rare combination of dry air, little light pollution, and high elevation makes it perfect for viewing galaxies. The Milky Way is most visible during moonless nights from mid-summer through early fall evenings.[24]

https://www.nps.gov/grsa/index.htm

11999 State Hwy 150, Mosca, CO 81146

719-378-6395

*Hours: Open 24/7 year-round! There are no reservations to make or limit on the number of visitors in the park and preserve, but there is currently limited capacity in the visitor center.*

*Basic Entrance Pass (good for up to seven consecutive days): Non-commercial Vehicle and Occupants (normal car) $25 / Oversized Vehicle or Large Van (15+ passengers, age 16+) $15 per person / Motorcycle and Riders $20*

# 48. Chimney Rock National Monument

## SOUTHEAST COLORADO

Chimney Rock National Monument is where culture and history are part of the adventure. A visit to this national monument takes you to the southern boundary of the San Juan Mountains. The area is an off-the-beaten-path archaeological site that gives you insight into the Ancient Puebloans of the Chaco Canyon. Seeing the Chaco culture with the San Juan National Forests background provides a perfect setting for discovering what Chimney Rock has to offer. Pass by the ancient homes and ceremonial structures, hike up to Chimney Rock, a quick half-mile from the base, and you are rewarded with 360-degree views of Colorado and New Mexico.[49]

Chimney Rock Interpretive Association

P.O. Box 1662, Pagosa Springs, CO 81147

Monument: 970-883-5359 *(from May 15–Sep 30)*

Reservations: 1 877-444-6777

CRIA Office: 970-731-7133

*Gate Opens: 9:00am–4:30pm (last tour at 3:00pm)*

*Self-Guided Tours: Adults $12 / Children (5–12) $6*

# 49. Farmer's Market

## SOUTHEAST COLORADO

Alamosa Farmers Market—This farmers market is located at State Ave. and 6th St. in Alamosa and is open every Saturday from July to October. The Alamosa Farmers Market includes local growers, certified dairy producers, and meat producers who offer organic, grass-fed beef, lamb, and yak. You'll also find craft and hygiene vendors, among others.[56]

. . .

www.alamosafarmersmarket.org

Corner of 6th St and State Ave, Alamosa, CO 81101

719-480-4365

Boulder Farmers Market—Recently named the "Best Farmers Market in the U.S.," Boulder Farmers Market is open every Saturday and Wednesday, from the first Saturday in April through the third Saturday in November. The markets feature everything from local fruits and vegetables, locally sourced crafts, and potted seedlings for the home gardener, to prepared foods from local bakeries, gourmet cheese, small-batch honey, and artisan salsas.[57]

www.bcfm.org

13th St, Boulder, CO 80302

303-910-2236

Greeley Farmers Market—Not just a farmers market, the Greeley Farmers Market has live entertainment, lectures from master gardeners, and informational booths. Operation is every Saturday from mid-May to October and every Wednesday from July to

September. They offer a wide variety of locally grown and produced food products, including in-season fresh produce, meats, honey, bread and other baked goods, roasted chilies, and specialty items from local artisans and crafters.[58]

greeleygov.com

902 7th Ave, Greeley, CO 80631

970-336-4219

• • •

Montrose Farmers Market—This year-round market located on S. Uncompahgre between Main Street & S. 1st Street brings together the produce and crafts from the Western Slope. You'll find locally made goodies such as baked goods, honey, jams, greenhouse produce, fresh farm eggs, locally produced meats, and handcrafted jewelry.[59]

https://www.colorado.com/farmers-markets/montrose-farmers-market

South 1st and Uncompahgre Montrose, CO 81401

970-249-0705

Larimer County Farmers Market—Dubbed the oldest Farmers Market in Northern Colorado, Larimer County Farmers Market is run by Colorado State University Master Gardeners. All products offered are grown, produced, or made by the local vendors. The market features the best vendor-produced fruits, honey, flowers, herbs, cheese, meats, jellies, and other agriculture-related products.[60]

www.larimercountyfm.org

200 W Oak St, Fort Collins, CO 80521

970-498-6000

Vail Farmers Market—Unlike other farmers markets, Vail Farmers Market opens on Sunday. It has more than 135 tents and a pleasing county-fair flair.

www.vailfarmersmarket.com

E Meadow Dr, Vail, CO 81657

# 50. Dude Ranches

## SOUTHEAST COLORADO

Dude ranches are oriented toward visitors or tourism, offering activities such as horseback riding, target shooting, and cattle sorting. Accommodation can range from rustic cabins to renovated five-star cabins.[48]

. . .

We've listed a few of our favorites below.

. . .

Vista Verde Ranch, Steamboat Springs

For a luxurious experience check out Vista Verde Ranch in Steamboat Springs. They've got a wellness program, horse clinics, fly fishing, cooking classes and wine tasting.

www.vistaverde.com 58000 Cowboy Way, Clark, CO 80428

970-879-3858

Cherokee Park Ranch, Livermore

Established in 1886, this historic Cherokee Park Ranch is pure bliss. Surrounded by Rocky Mountain wilderness, you won't feel like you are less than 100 miles away from the Denver Airport. Set along the Cache la Poudre River, families can enjoy raft trips, tubing, boat trips, or picnic lunches.

www.cherokeeparkranch.com 436 Cherokee Hills Dr, Livermore, CO 80536

970-493-6522

Latigo Ranch, Kremmling

Latigo Ranch offers top-notch horseback riding. In addition, it is surrounded by national forest and an open meadow. Both summer and winter offer activities that are ideal for families or adult only trips.

latigoranch.com 201 County Rd 1911, Kremmling, CO 80459

970-724-9008

• • •

Rainbow Trout Ranch, Antonito

www.rainbowtroutranch.com 1484 Forest Service Rd 250, Antonito, CO 81120

719-376-2440

# Bucket List Tracker

| Date(s) | Location/Activity |
|---------|-------------------|
|         |                   |
|         |                   |
|         |                   |
|         |                   |
|         |                   |
|         |                   |
|         |                   |
|         |                   |
|         |                   |
|         |                   |
|         |                   |
|         |                   |
|         |                   |

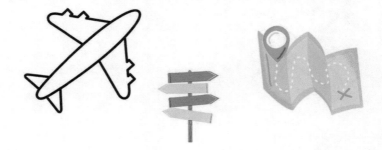

# Bucket List Tracker

| Date(s) | Location/Activity |
|---------|-------------------|
|         |                   |
|         |                   |
|         |                   |
|         |                   |
|         |                   |
|         |                   |
|         |                   |
|         |                   |
|         |                   |
|         |                   |
|         |                   |
|         |                   |
|         |                   |
|         |                   |

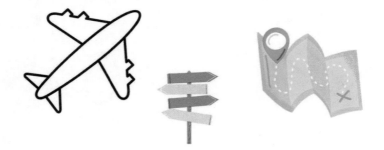

# Bucket List Tracker

| Date(s) | Location/Activity |
|---------|-------------------|
|         |                   |
|         |                   |
|         |                   |
|         |                   |
|         |                   |
|         |                   |
|         |                   |
|         |                   |
|         |                   |
|         |                   |
|         |                   |
|         |                   |
|         |                   |
|         |                   |

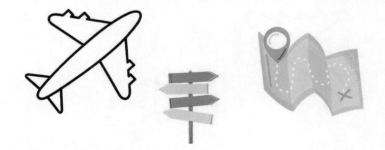

# Bucket List Tracker

| Date(s) | Location/Activity |
|---------|-------------------|
|         |                   |
|         |                   |
|         |                   |
|         |                   |
|         |                   |
|         |                   |
|         |                   |
|         |                   |
|         |                   |
|         |                   |
|         |                   |
|         |                   |
|         |                   |

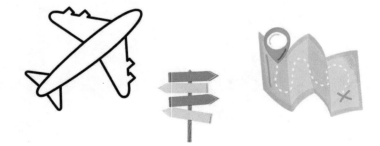

# Endnotes

1. https://www.britannica.com/place/Rocky-Mountain-National-Park

2. https://www.nps.gov/romo/planyourvisit/holzwarth-historic-site.htm

3. https://enosmills.com/

4. https://www.visitgrandcounty.com/trips/itineraries/trail-ridge-road

5. https://en.wikipedia.org/wiki/Garden_of_the_Gods

6. https://www.visitcos.com/things-to-do/

7. https://www.pikes-peak.com/attractions/cave-of-the-winds/

8. https://www.visitcos.com/directory/colorado-springs-fine-arts-center-at-colorado-college/

9. https://denverpublicart.org/

10. https://en.wikipedia.org/wiki/Denver_Art_Museum

11. https://mcadenver.org/

12. https://www.botanicgardens.org/york-street

13. https://www.botanicgardens.org/chatfield-farms

14. https://www.botanicgardens.org/other-locations/plains-conservation-center

15. https://www.botanicgardens.org/other-locations/mount-goliath

16.  https://mesaverdecountry.com/things-to-do/mesa-verde-national-park/

17.  https://www.businessinsider.com/aspen-colorado-most-expensive-ski-town-prices-photos

18. https://www.cntraveler.com/story/where-to-eat-stay-and-play-in-aspen-colorado

19. https://www.cntraveler.com/story/where-to-eat-stay-and-play-in-aspen-colorado

20. https://en.wikipedia.org/wiki/Aspen,_Colorado

21. https://aspenchamber.org/plan-trip/how-to/get-here/by-air

22. https://aspenchamber.org/plan-trip/trip-highlights/maroon-bells

23. https://www.aspensnowmass.com/plan-your-stay/maroon-bells

24.  https://www.doi.gov/blog/great-sand-dunes-national-park-and-preserve

25. https://silvertonmountain.com/

26. https://www.durango.org/

27. https://www.ski.com/how-to-get-to-vail

28.  https://www.hikevail.net/trails/more-difficult-trails/booth-lake-trail

29. https://www.nps.gov/dino/index.htm

30. www.visitbreck.com

31. https://gobreck.com/breckenridge-tips/

32.  https://www.bouldercoloradousa.com/meetings-and-groups/meeting-transportation/

33. https://www.bouldercolorado.gov/

34. https://coloradowildernessridesandguides.com/rock-climbing/rock-climbing-boulders-flatirons/

35. https://www.colorado.com/byways/peak-to-peak

36. https://www.colorado.com/articles/Black-Canyon-Gunnison-National-Park

37. https://www.nps.gov/blca/index.htm

38. https://steamboatsprings.net/131/Howelsen-Hill-Ski-Area

39. https://en.wikipedia.org/wiki/Steamboat_Springs,_Colorado

40. https://www.steamboat.com/things-to-do/activities/hiking/fish-creek-falls

41. https://www.visitftcollins.com/maps-info/neighborhoods/old-town/

42. https://www.larimer.org/naturalresources/parks/permits

43. https://stateparks.com/lory_state_park_in_colorado.html

44. https://www.rivers.gov/

45. https://visitglenwood.com/area-info/directions/

46. https://www.fs.usda.gov/visit/browns-canyon-national-monument

47. https://www.colorado.com/articles/plan-your-visit-browns-canyon-national-monument

48. https://en.wikipedia.org/wiki/Guest_ranch

49. https://www.chimneyrockco.org/

50. https://cityofcoloradosprings.aluvii.com/store/shop/

productdetails?id=1&productId=1

51. https://www.colorado.com/cities-and-towns/lake-city

52. https://www.colorado.com/cities-and-towns/ouray

53. https://en.wikipedia.org/wiki/Silverton,_Colorado

54. https://www.durango.com/san-juan-national-forest/

55. https://en.wikipedia.org/wiki/U.S._Route_550

56. http://www.alamosafarmersmarket.org/

57. https://www.colorado.com/farmers-markets/boulder-farmers-market

58. https://www.colorado.com/farmers-markets/greeley-farmers-market-depot

59. https://www.colorado.com/farmers-markets/montrose-farmers-market

60. https://cofarmersmarkets.org/markets/larimer-county-farmers-market/

61. https://en.wikipedia.org/wiki/Mount_Evans

62. https://en.wikipedia.org/wiki/Argo_Gold_Mine_and_Mill

63. https://royalgorgebridge.com/hours-directions/

64. https://en.wikipedia.org/wiki/Sangre_de_Cristo_Mountains

65. https://www.uncovercolorado.com/sangre-de-cristo-mountains/

66. https://www.nps.gov/flfo/index.htm

67. https://www.florissantfossilquarry.com/

# Photo Credits

Silverton & Old West Towns

https://search.creativecommons.org/photos/11f2a264-8823-4069-b204-c7349d05ba37

"Ghost Town of the West, Silverton, Colorado" by gloria.manna is licensed with CC BY-ND 2.0. To view a copy of this license, visit https://creativecommons.org/licenses/by-nd/2.0/

Browns Canyon National Monument https://search.creativecommons.org/photos/9374781a-c23d-4c6b-858d-4194617e77c2

"Browns Canyon National Monument" by mypubliclands is licensed with CC BY 2.0. To view a copy of this license, visit https://creativecommons.org/licenses/by/2.0/

Skyline Drive

https://search.creativecommons.org/photos/bf755b90-ff2c-41eb-be22-e1c35a8d4852

"Skyline Drive" by simonmgc is licensed with CC BY-ND 2.0. To view a copy of this license, visit https://creativecommons.org/licenses/by-nd/2.0/

New Belgium Brewing Company

https://search.creativecommons.org/photos/71e587b7-ffd6-41b5-b28a-cb1bd245af4d

Colorado Springs

Argo Mill and Tunnel

Colorado Springs Fine Arts Center

Denver Art Museum

Museum of Contemporary Art Denver